We hope you enjoy coloring this book.

Download some extra

free coloring patterns

and get news of upcoming books at

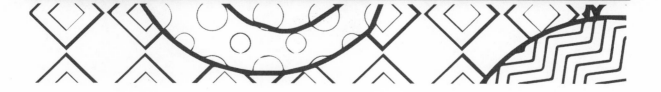

www.scribblepresscoloring.com/free-download

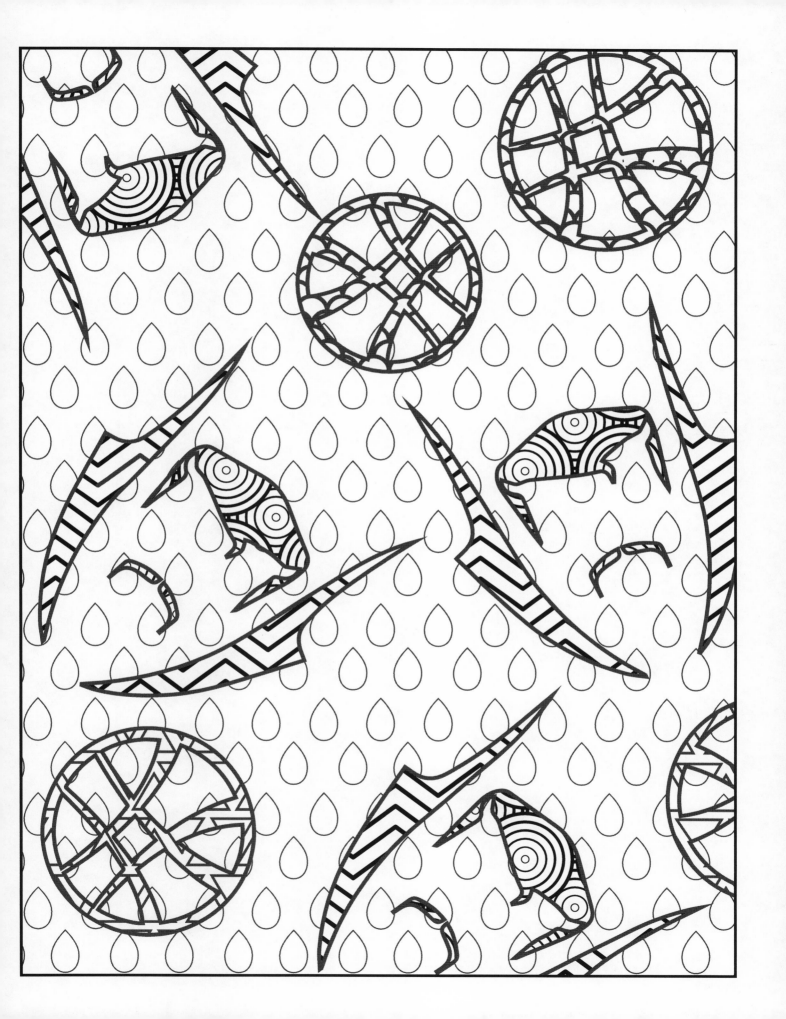

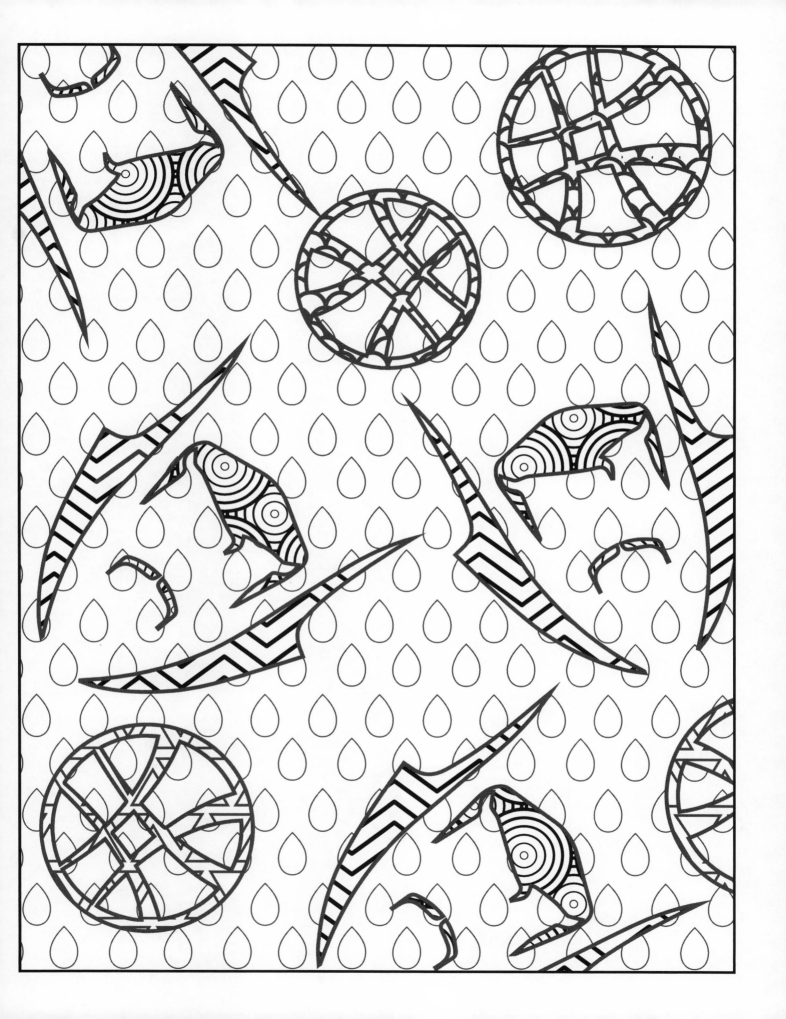

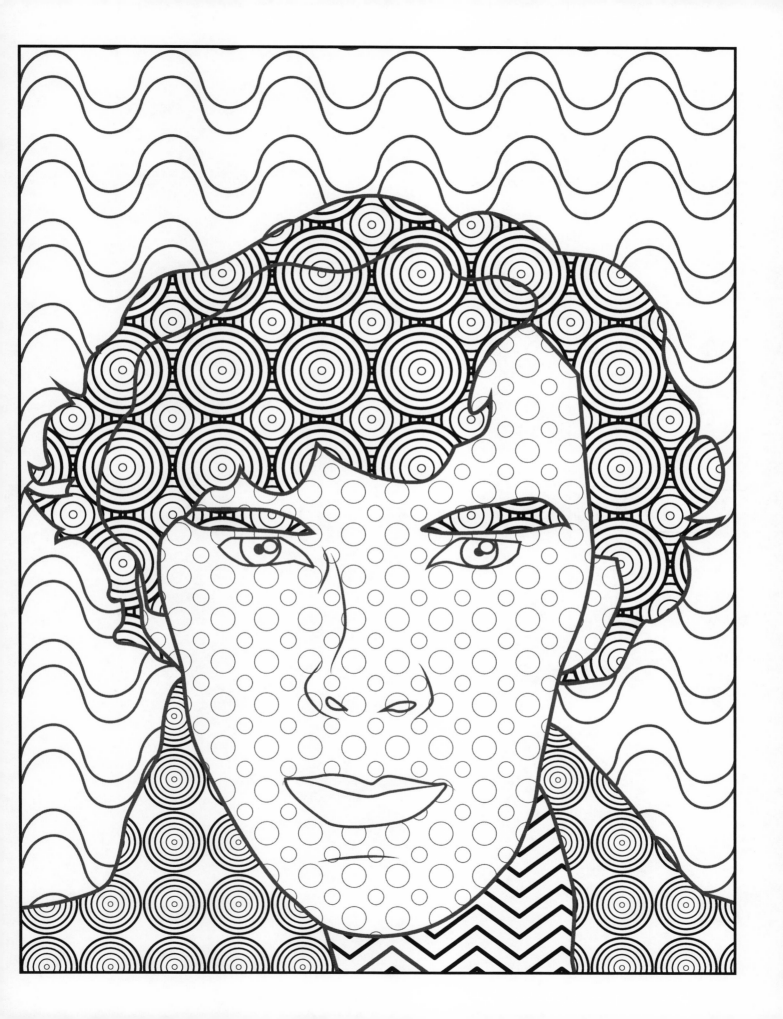

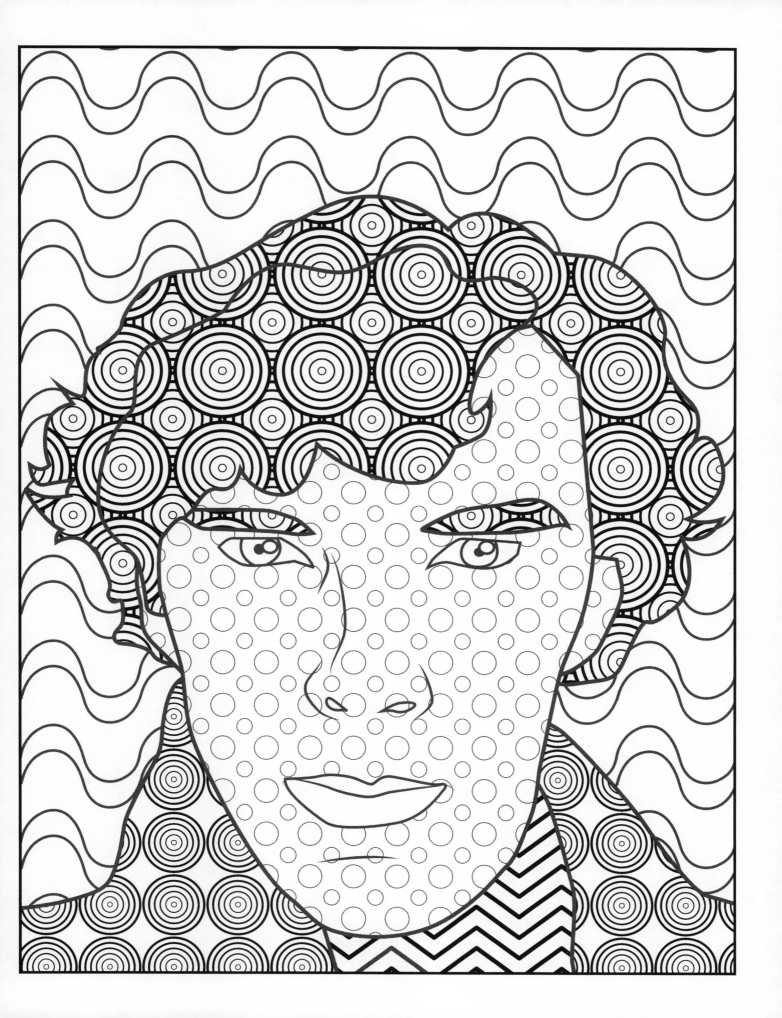

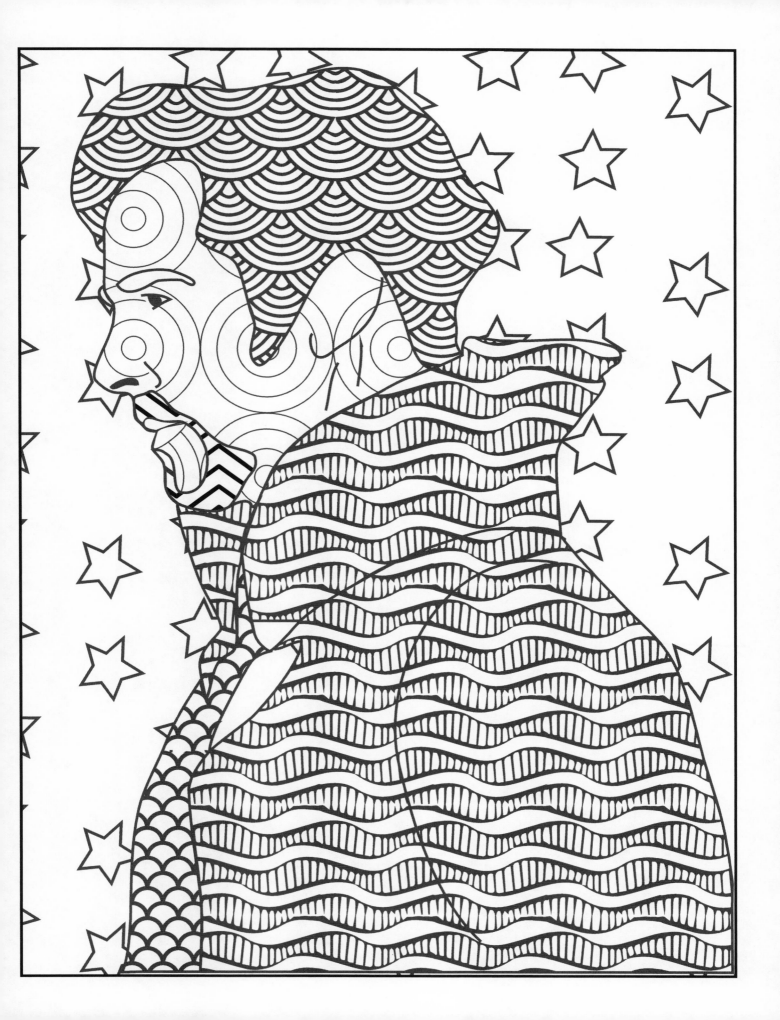

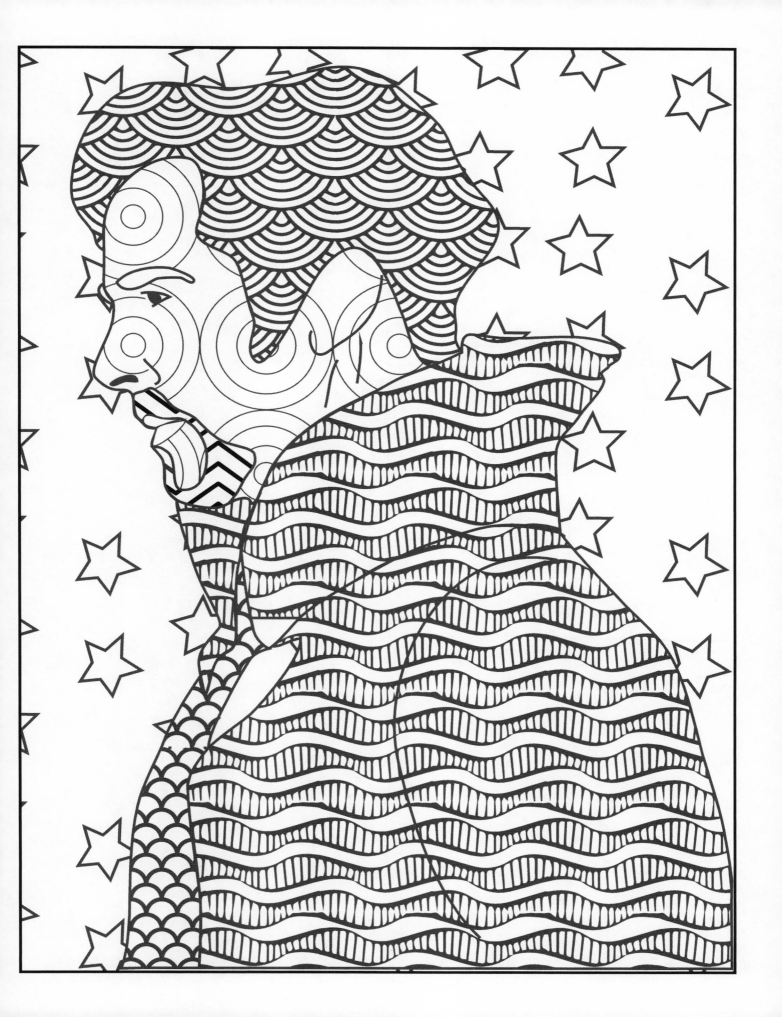

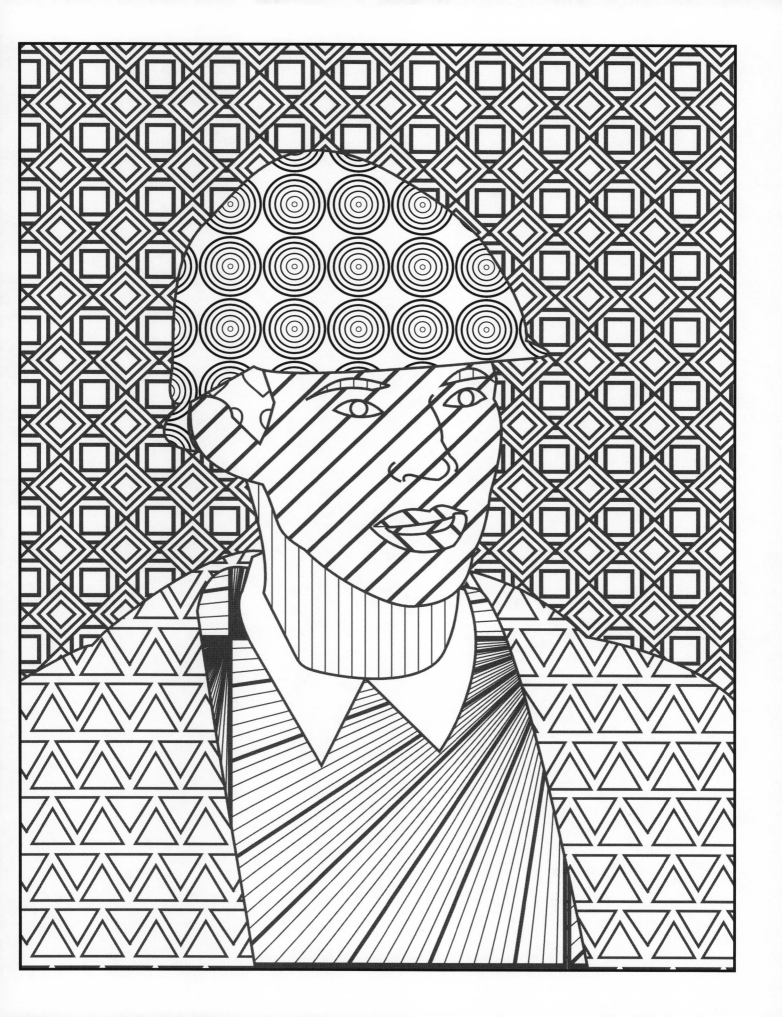

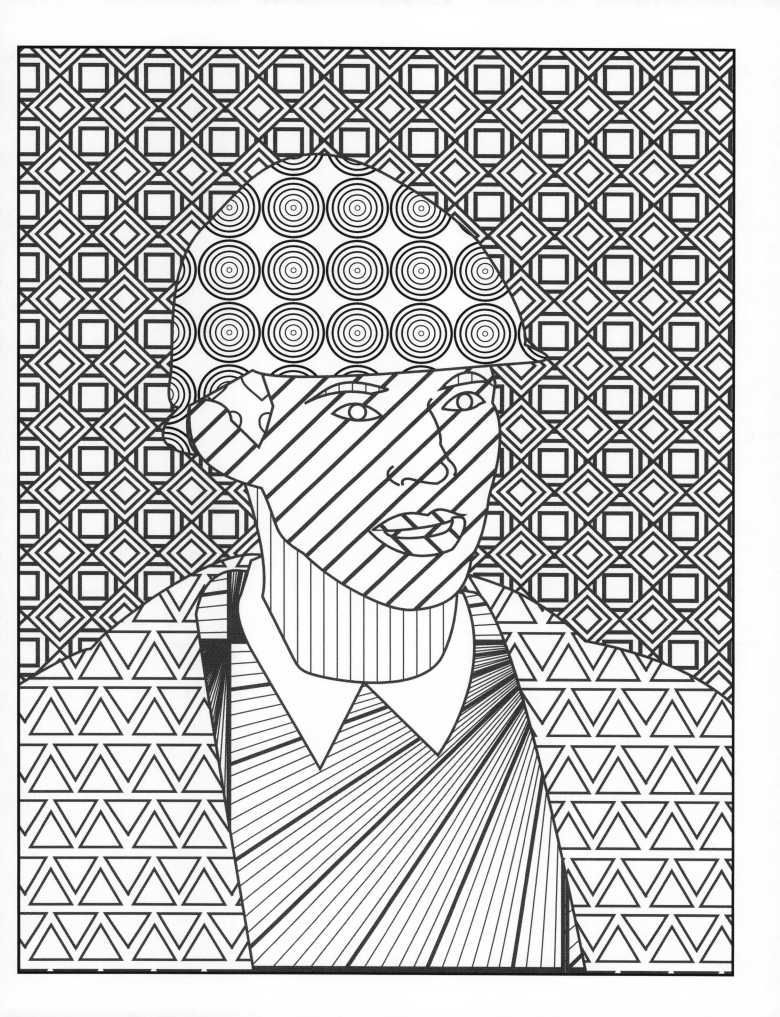

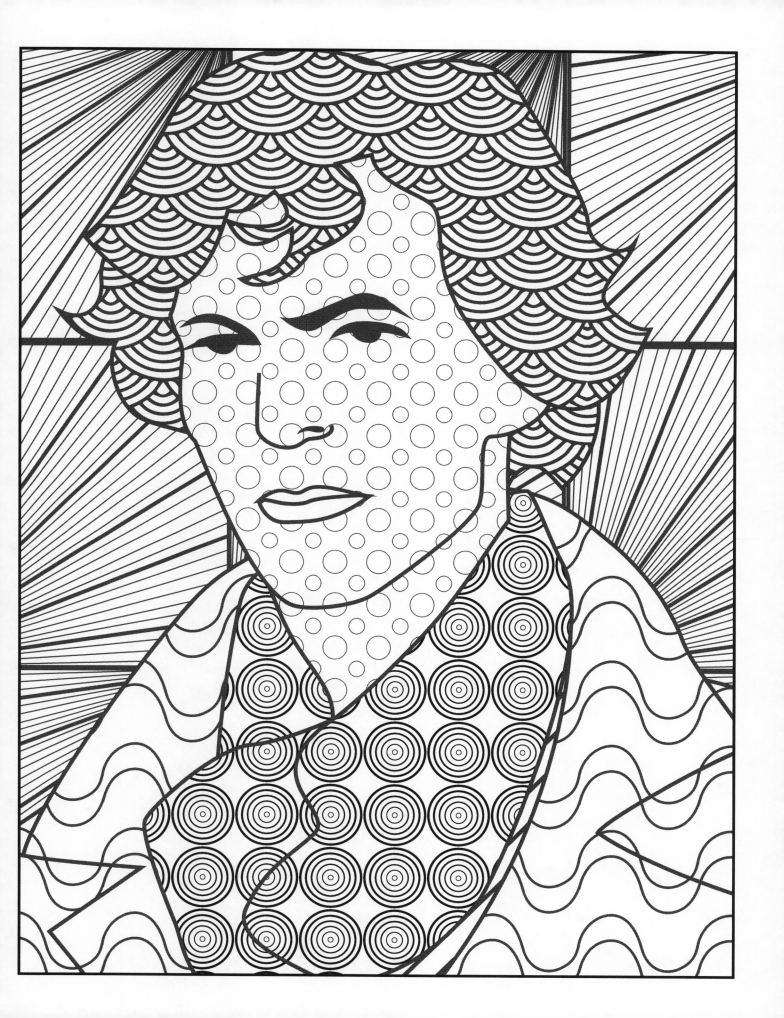

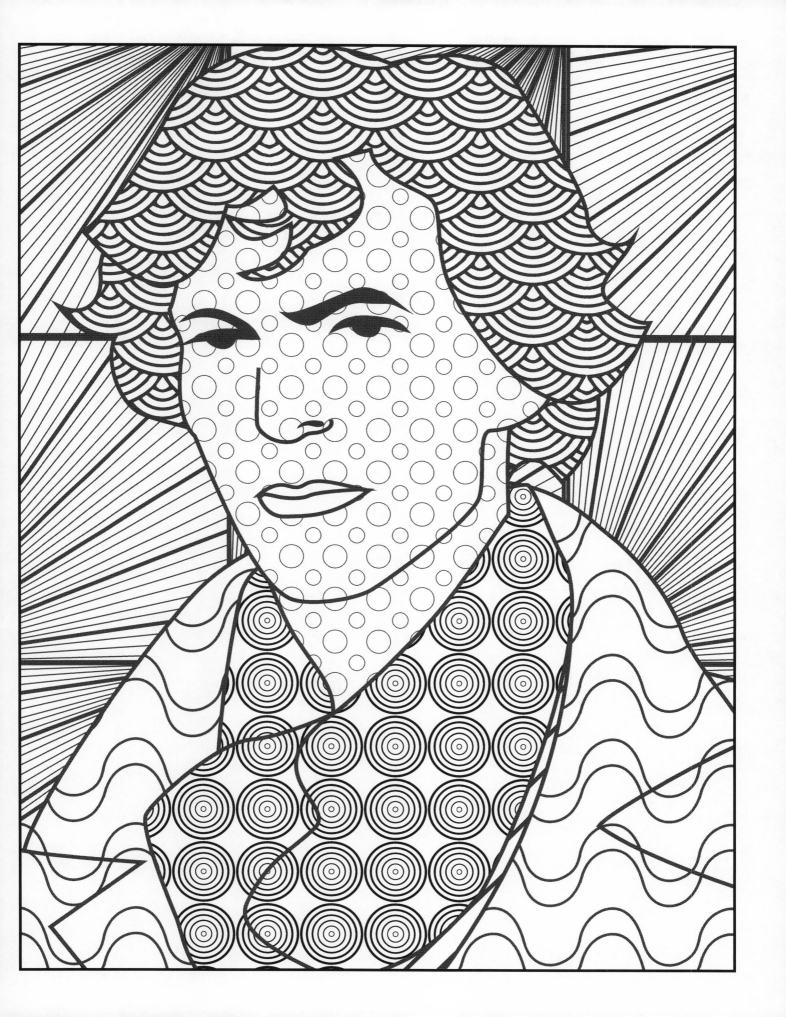

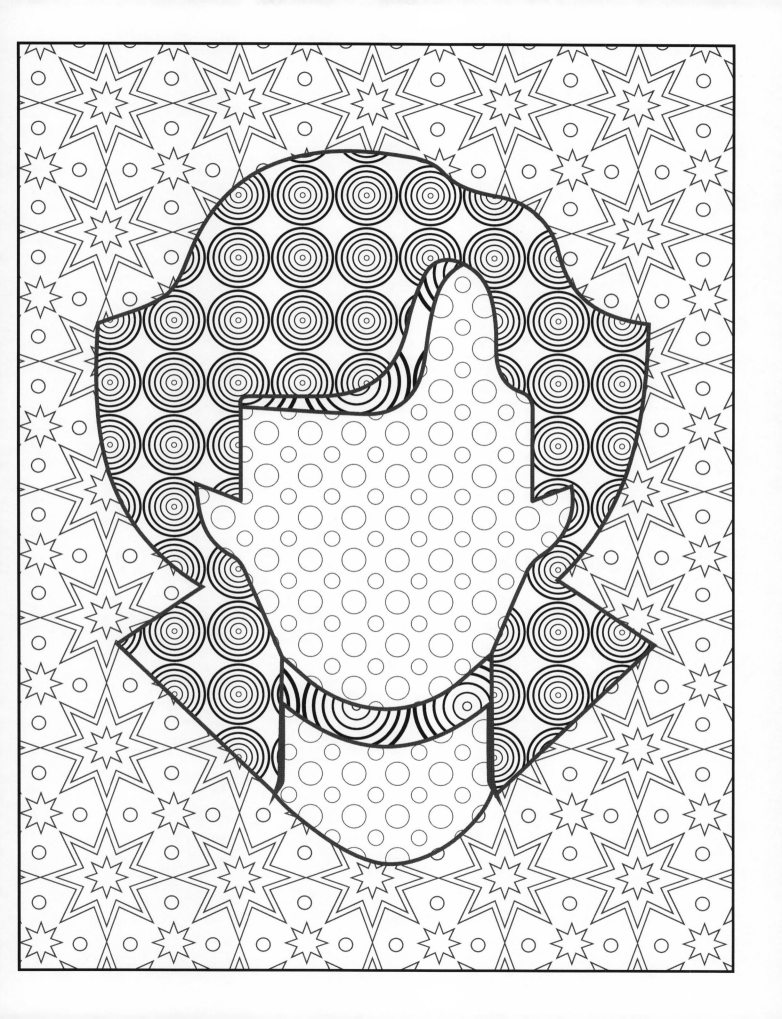

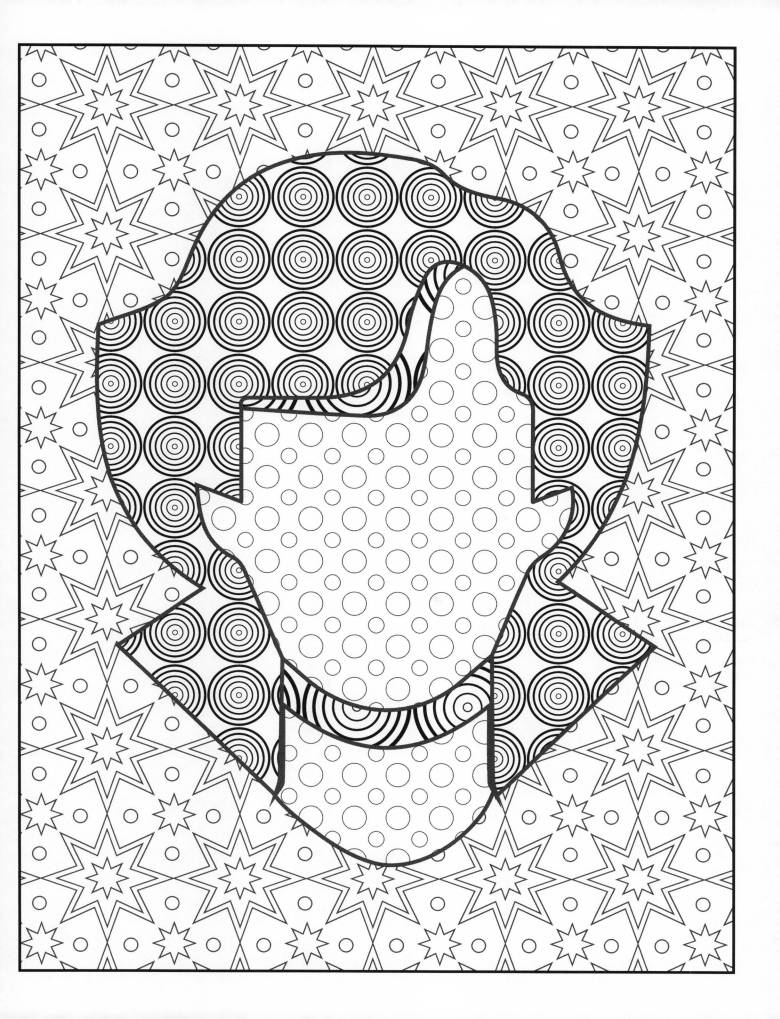

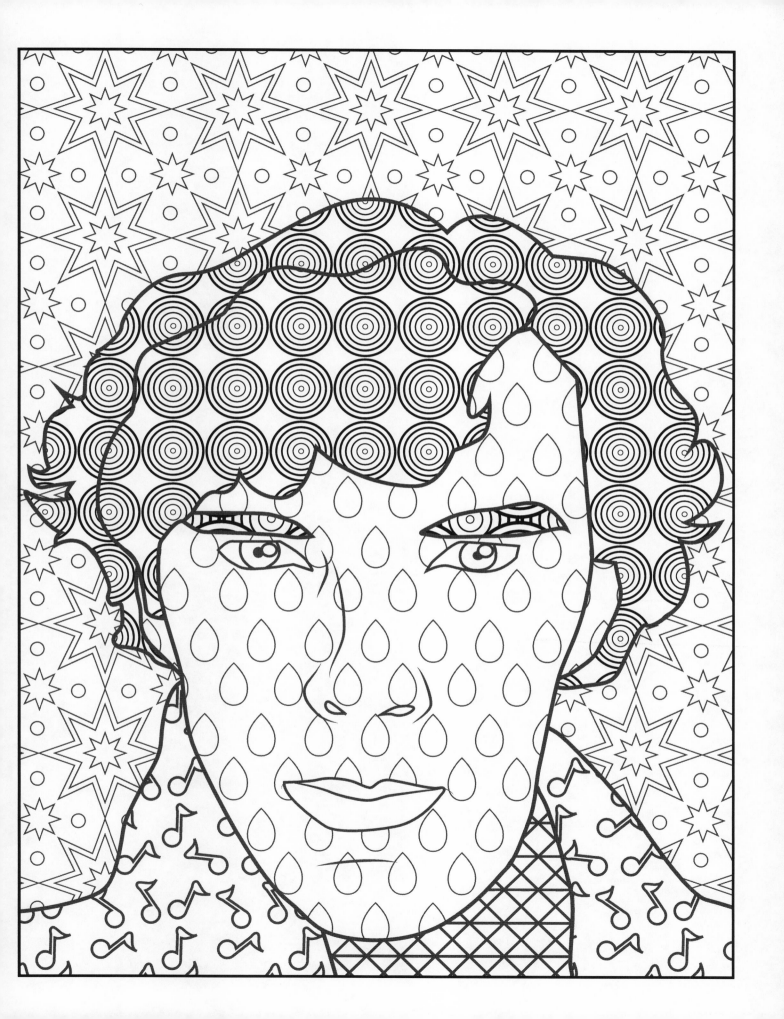

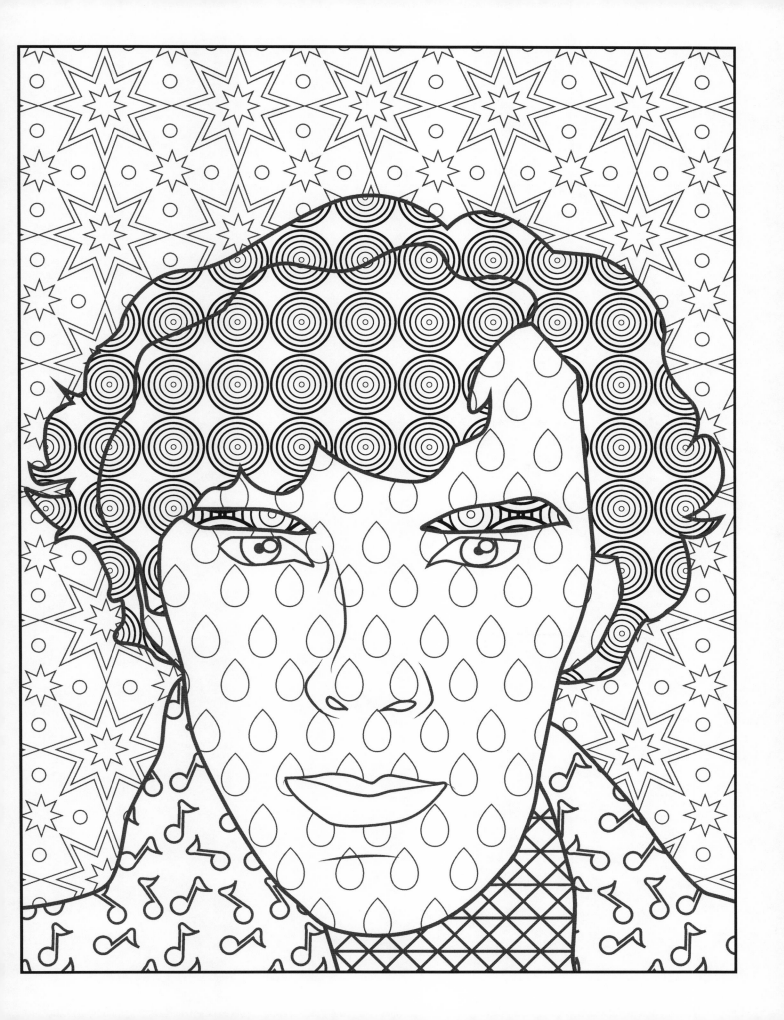

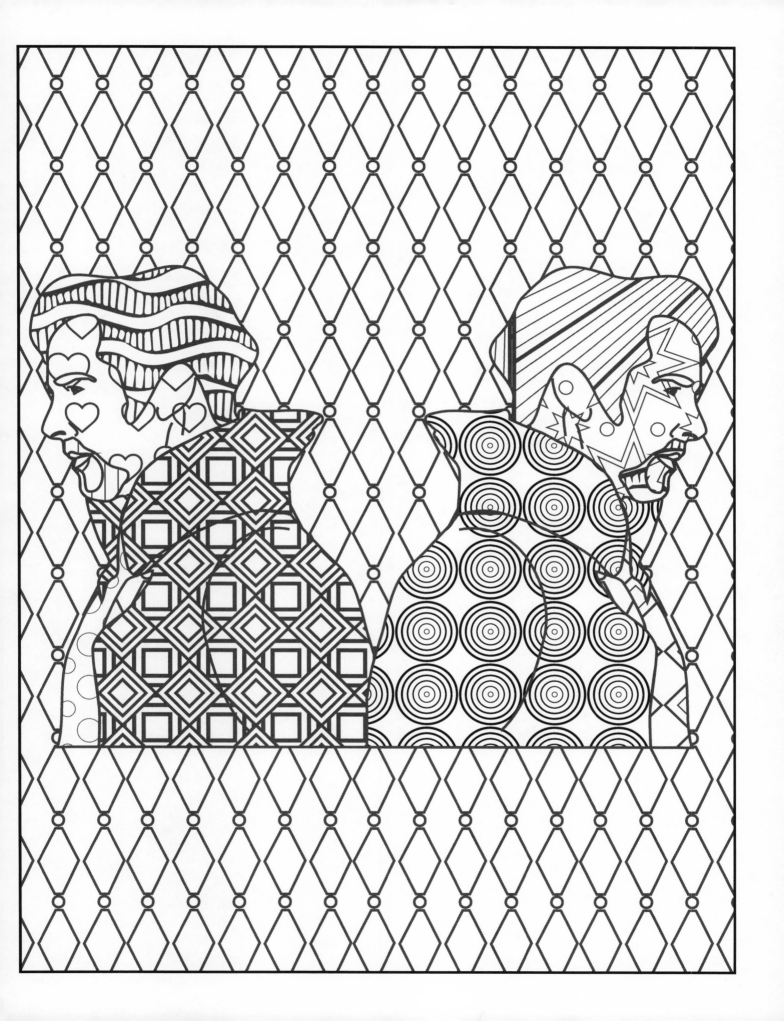

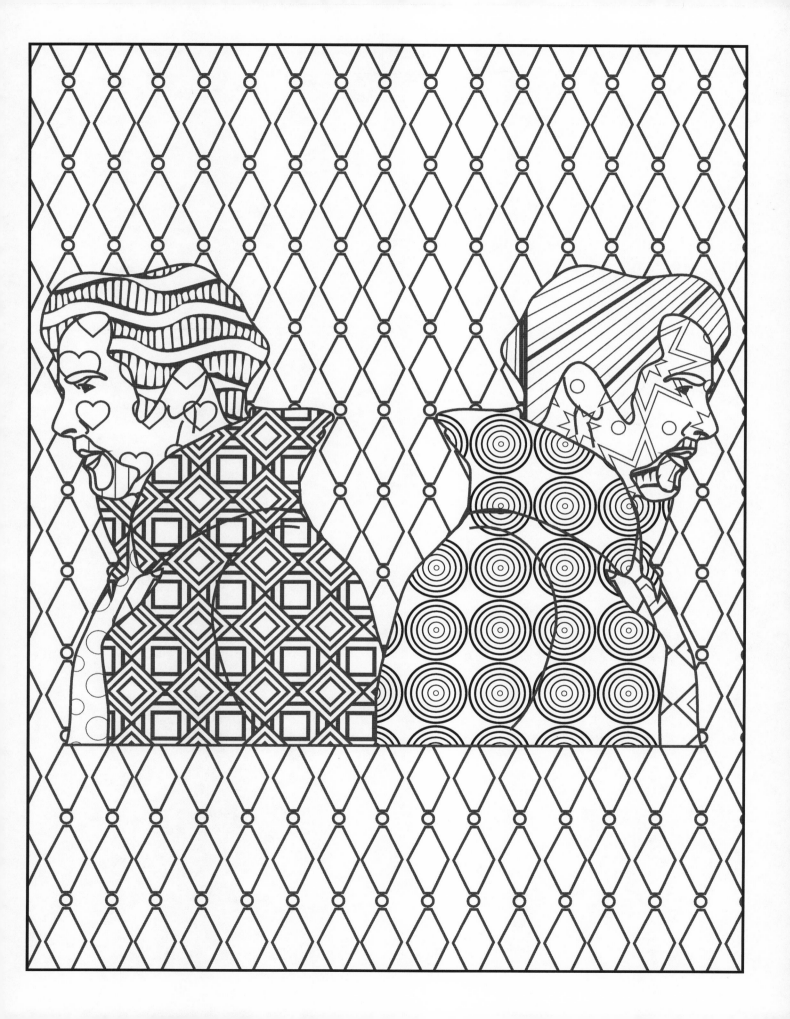

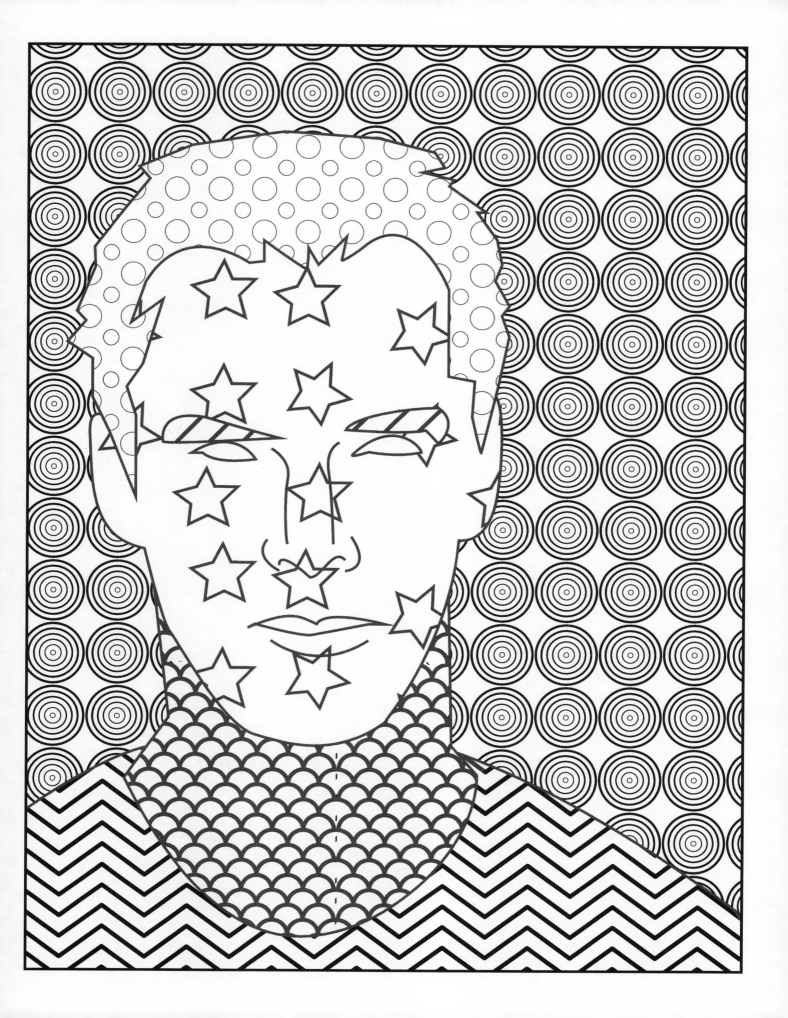

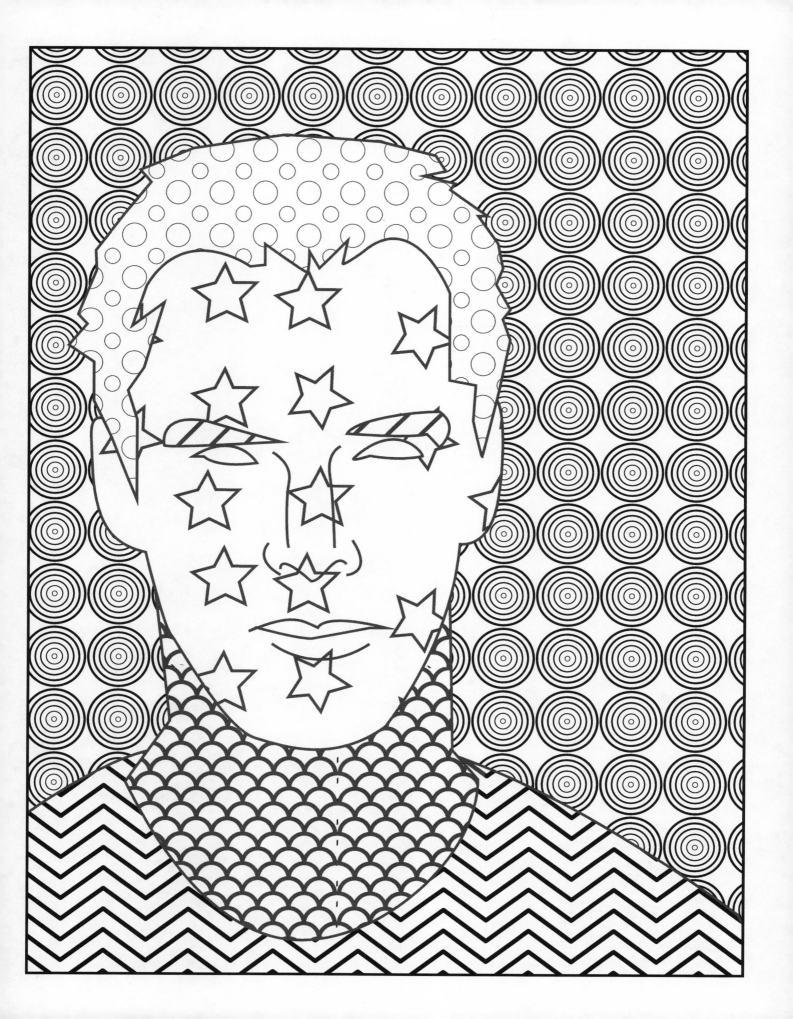

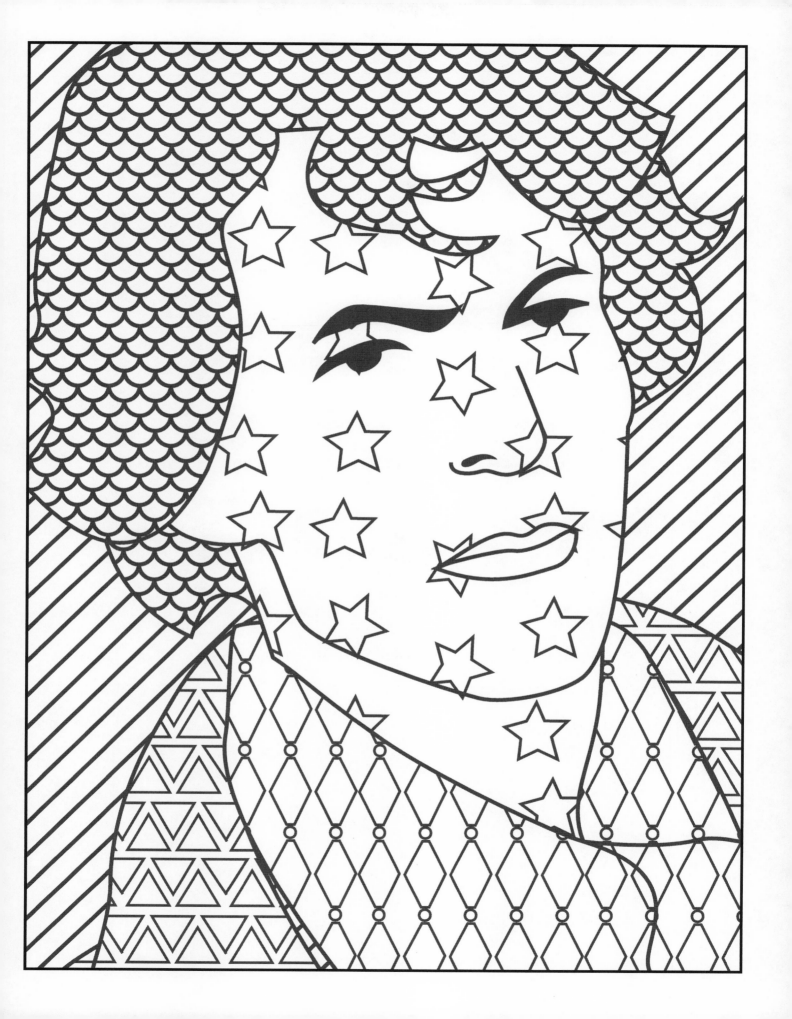

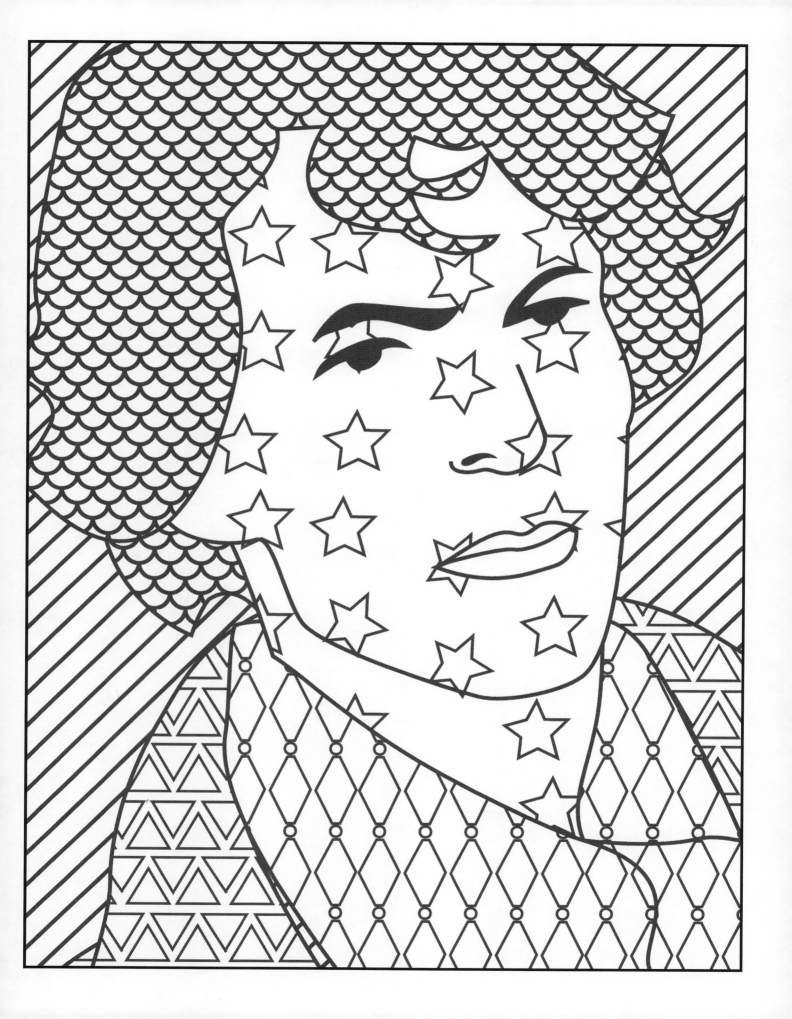

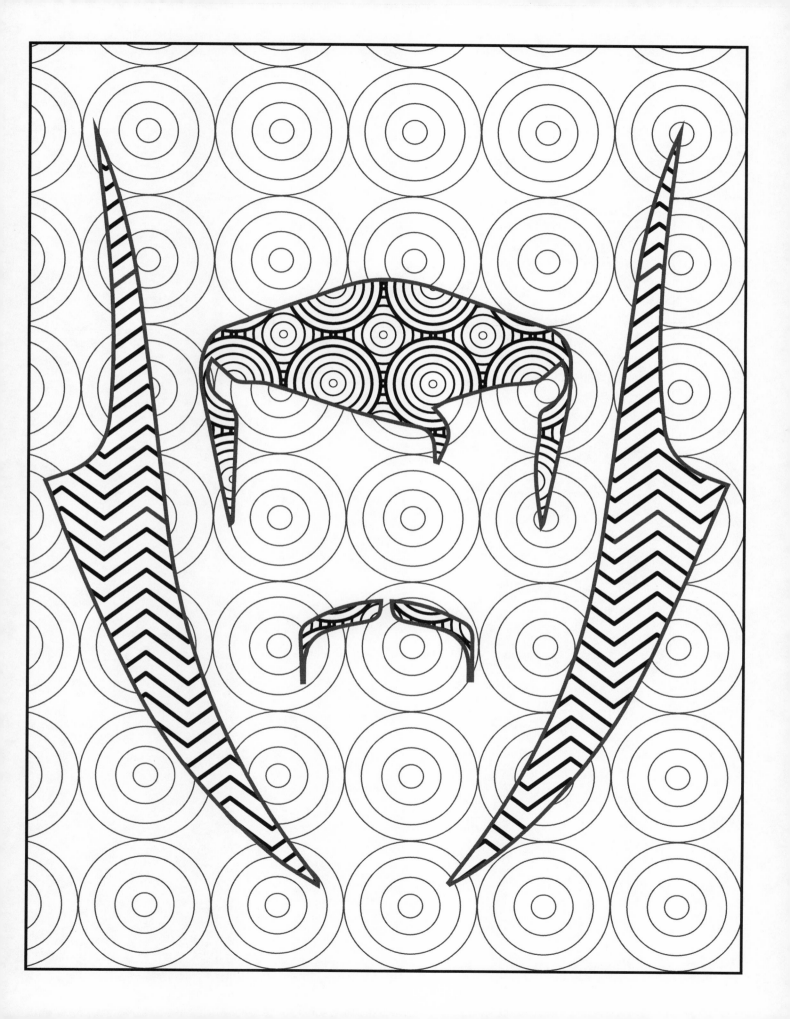

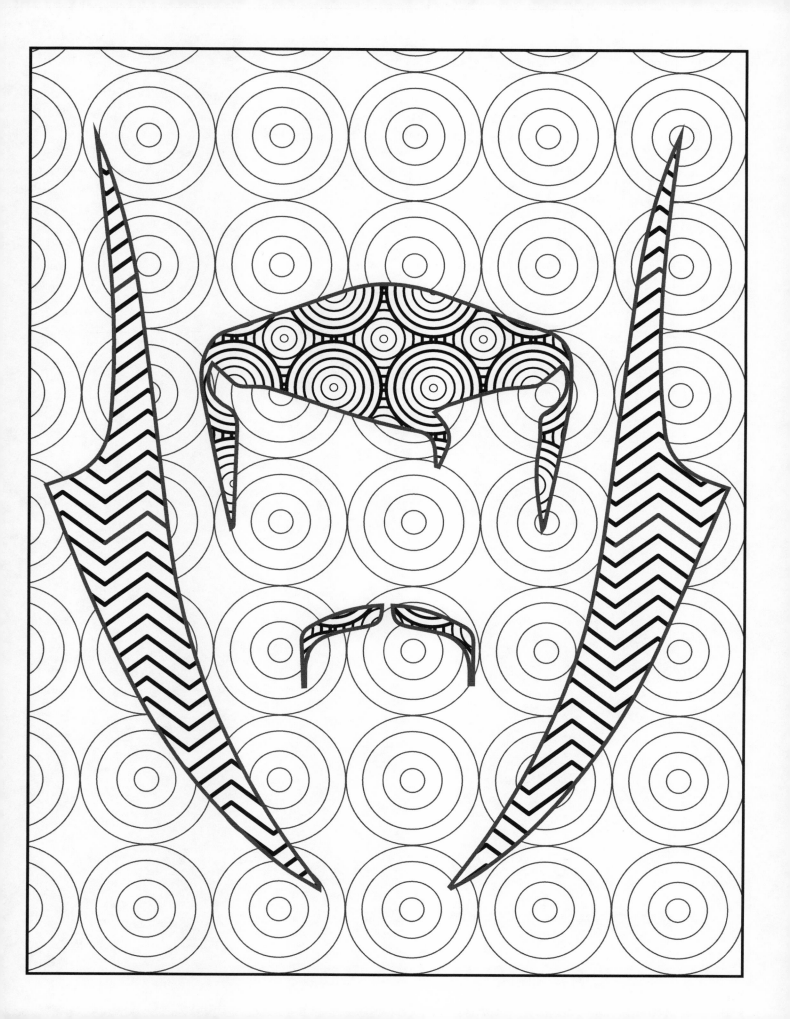

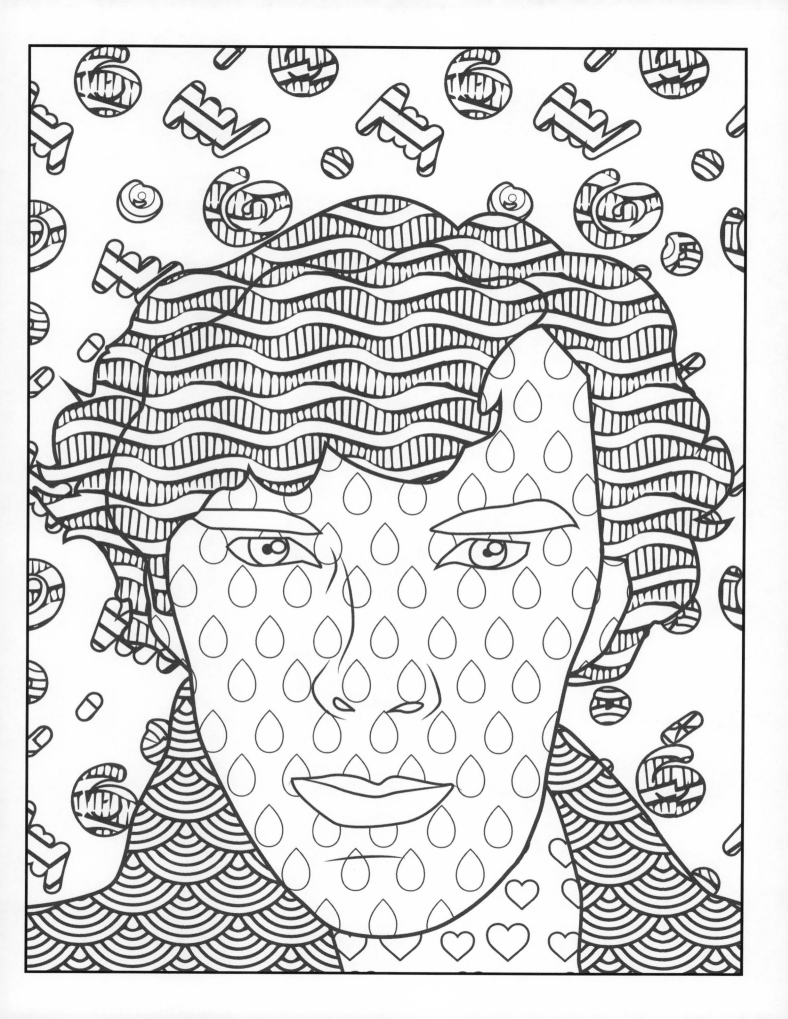

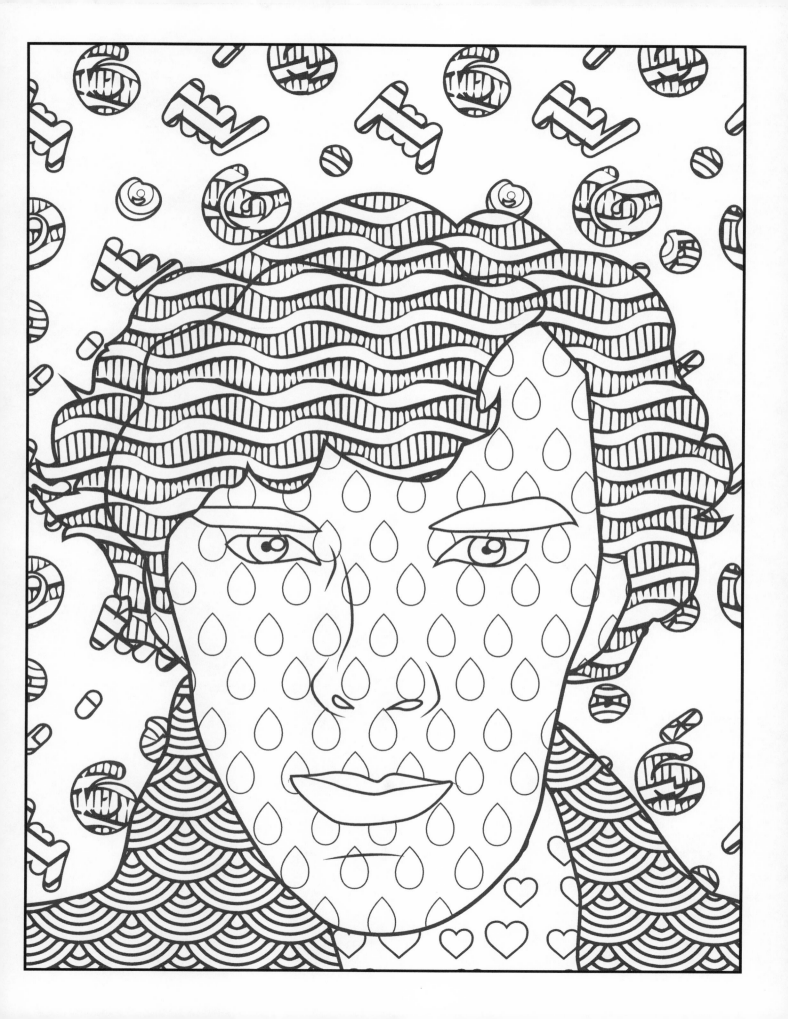

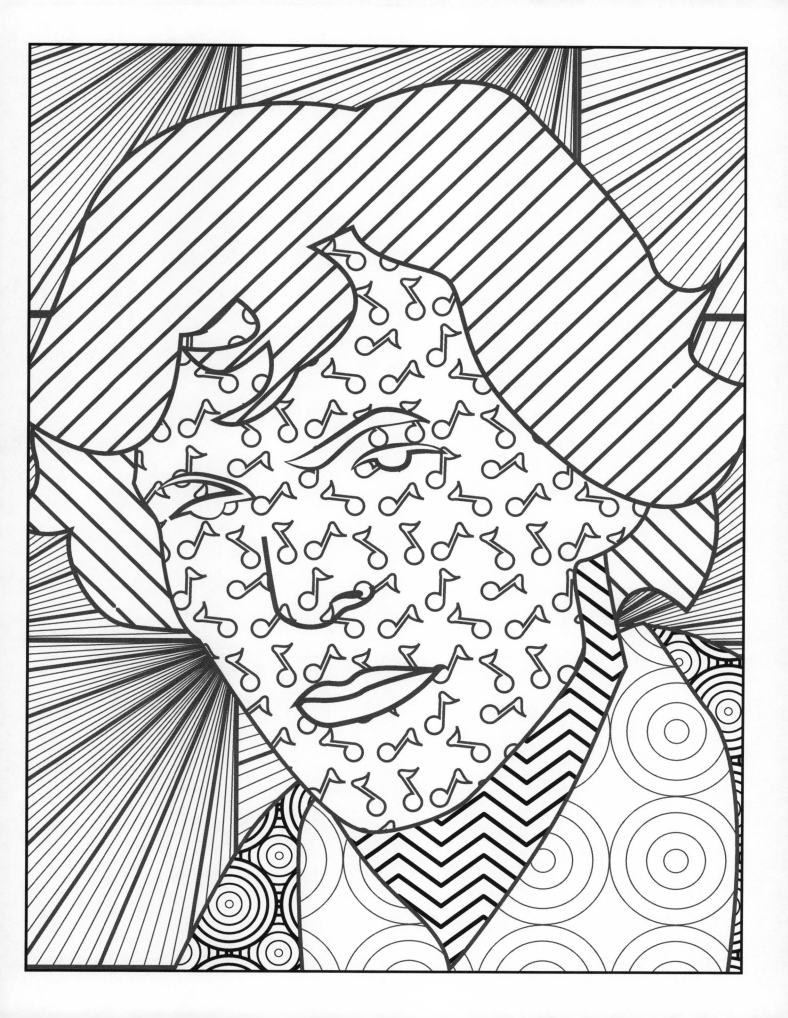

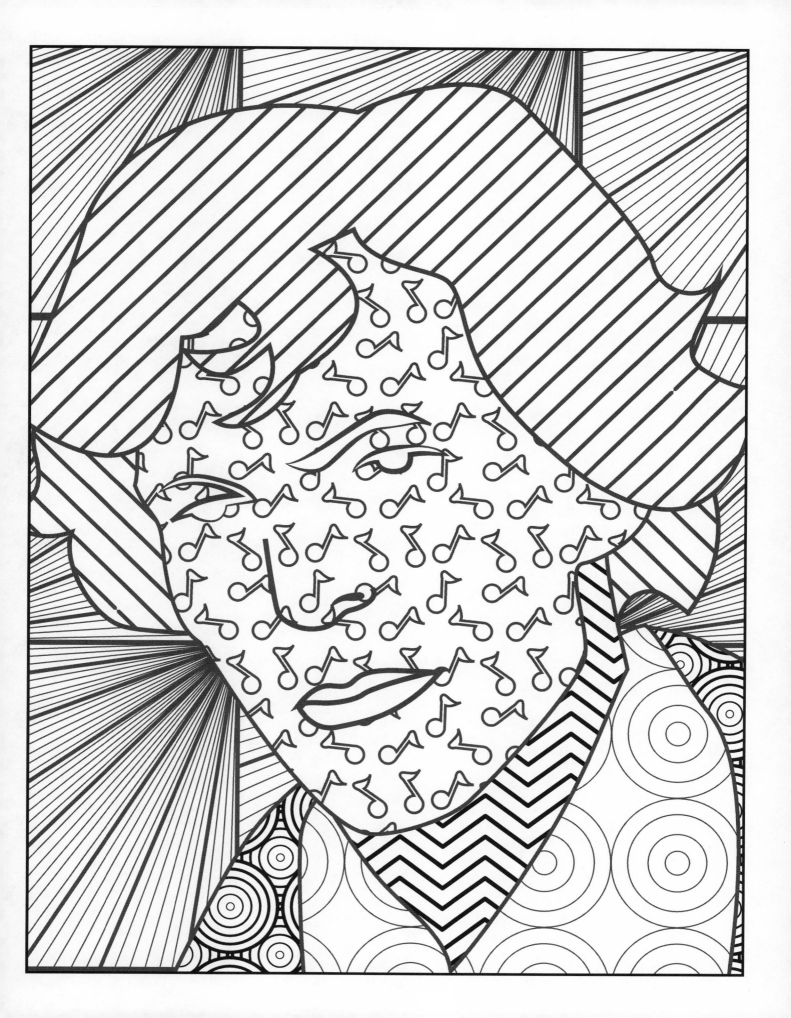

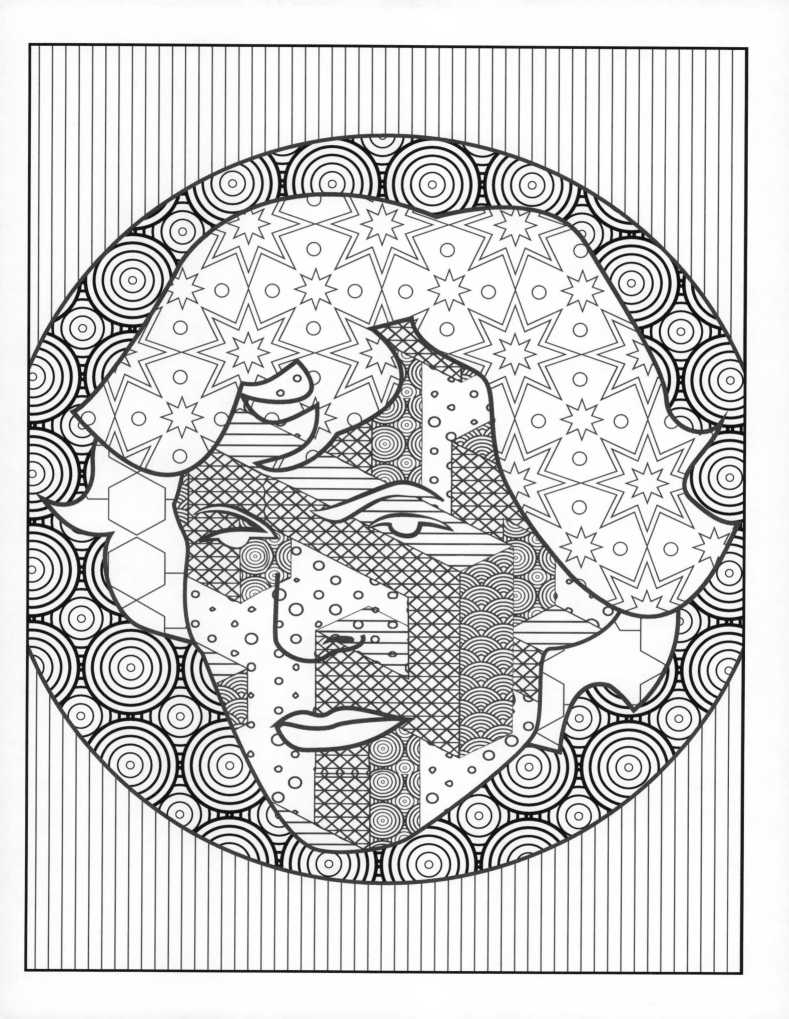

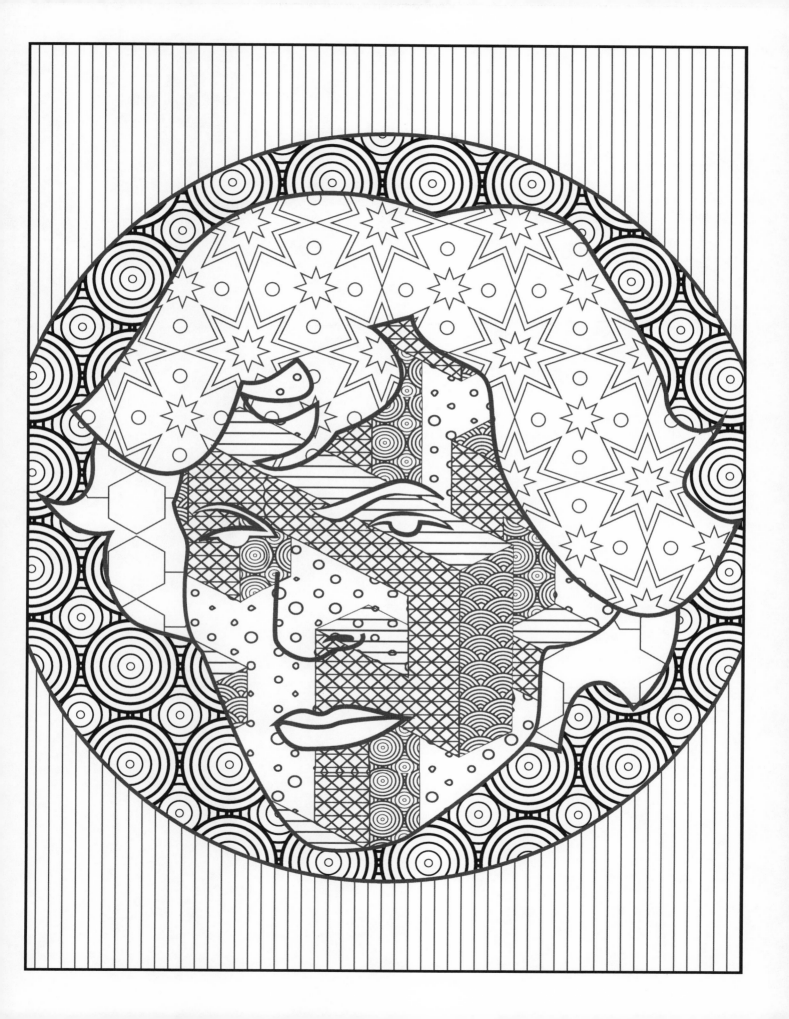

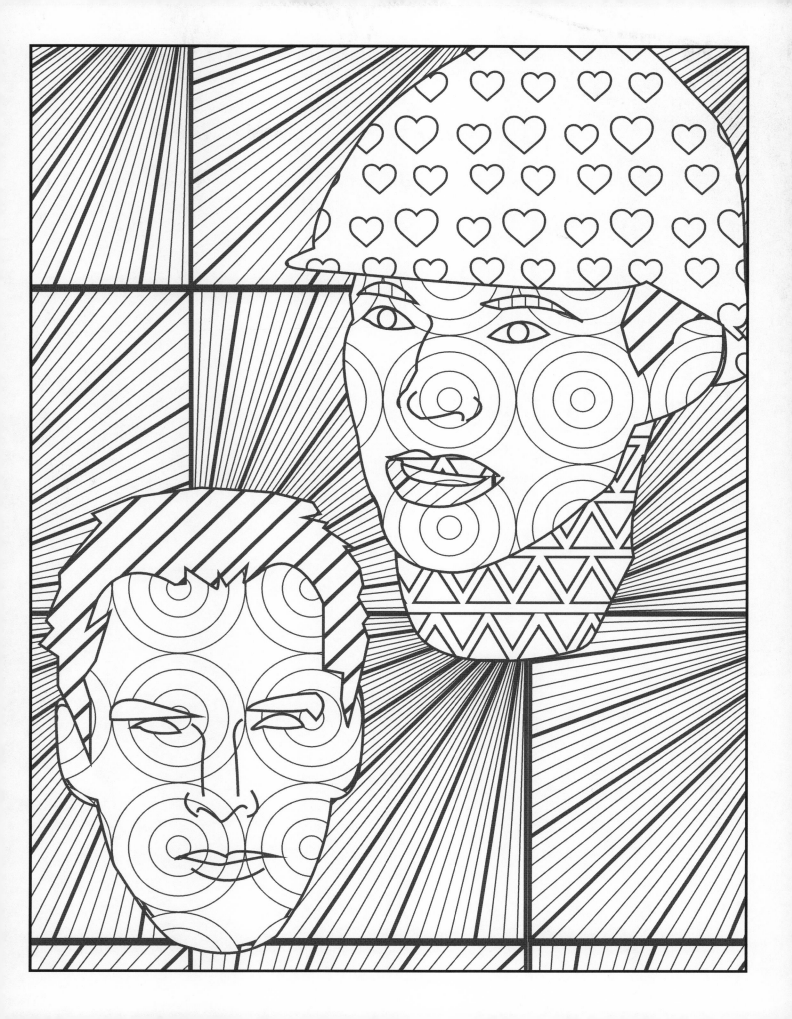

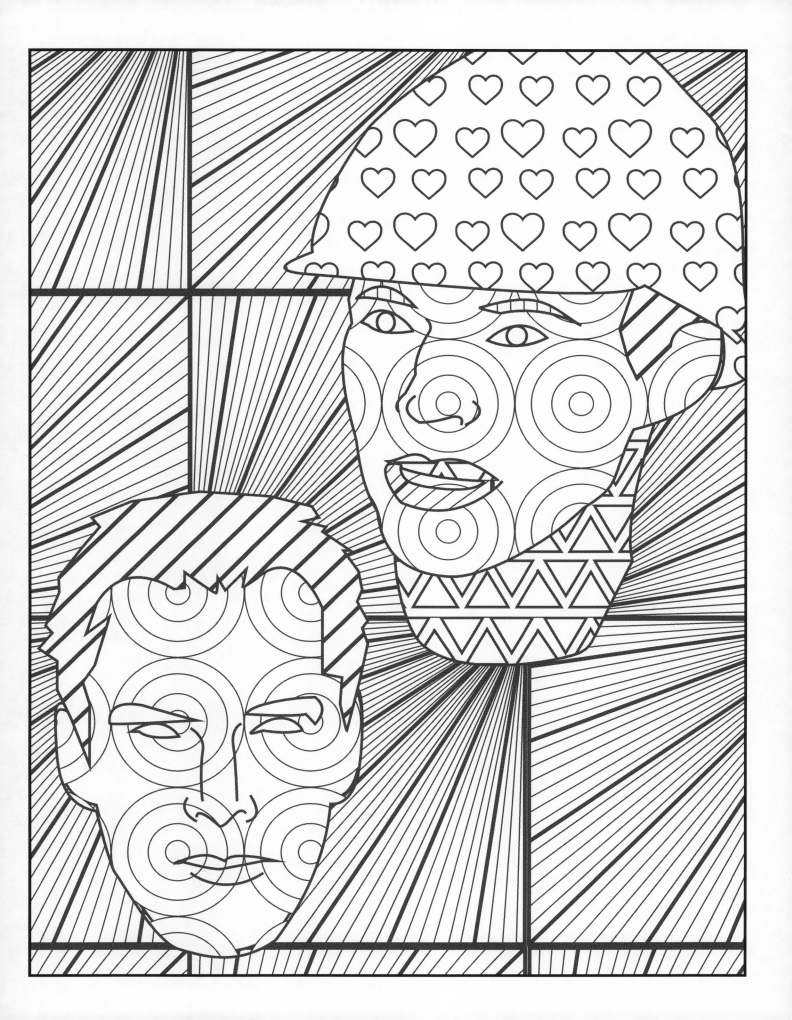

Manufactured by Amazon.ca
Bolton, ON

22170950R00037